Drawings

from Delta

to DMZ

from the

Sketchbooks of

Charles Waterhouse

Vietnamese Soldier

"Vietnamese ARVN wounded by VC in Delta."

VIETNAM SKETCHBOOK
Drawings from Delta to DMZ

by Charles Waterhouse

Charles E. Tuttle Company: Publishers
Rutland, Vermont   *Tokyo, Japan*

Representatives
Continental Europe: BOXERBOOKS, INC., *Zurich*
British Isles: PRENTICE-HALL INTERNATIONAL, INC., *London*
Australasia: PAUL FLESCH & CO., PTY. LTD., *Melbourne*
Canada: M. G. HURTIG LTD., *Edmonton*

Published by the Charles E. Tuttle Company, Inc.
of Rutland, Vermont and Tokyo, Japan
with editorial offices at
Suido 1-chome, 2–6, Bunkyo-ku, Tokyo, Japan

Copyright in Japan, 1968
by Charles E. Tuttle Co., Inc.

Library of Congress Catalog Card No. 68-21114

First printing, 1968

PRINTED IN JAPAN

This book of sketches
is dedicated to the many fine people
I had the privilege of meeting in
Vietnam, from all the services—
but especially my Marines...

INTRODUCTION

The drawings in this book were selected from 473 sketches I made in South Vietnam in March, 1967. They were made at all hours of the day—from the paddies and rivers of the Mekong Delta to the hills and foxholes on the DMZ—on land, sea, and in the air. I had received an invitation on the behalf of the Secretary of the Navy from Rear Admiral Henry L. Miller, Chief of Information, Department of the Navy, to document the activities of the United States Navy and the United States Marine Corps in South Vietnam for the Combat Art Collections of the USN and the USMC. I had been selected by chairman George Gray and the Navy Art Cooperation Liaison Committee (NACAL) of the New York City Salmagundi Club, the oldest professional art club in the United States, founded in 1871.

Since I normally work in the warmth and security of my New Jersey studio illustrating stories for magazines and books, I was a little reluctant to commit myself; however, two things made up my mind. First, I had been asked to join a small select group of artists who had covered military actions from the Civil War up through the Korean conflict, with names like Winslow Homer, Frederic Remington, Harvey Dunn, W. J. Aylward, Tom Lovell, Steven R. Kidd, and others. To be a member of such company proved irresistible. But the second reason was much more important. It was a chance to repay in some measure a debt to the USMC and to show my support for all our men in Vietnam. I could not carry a rifle for them, but if drawings could help, I was their man.

6

But first I had to convince myself that I was only a spectator, which in a way was helped by the fact that I left my home in a raging snow storm, boarded a jet, and after a matter of hours arrived in a never-never land where the temperature was in the high 90's and every one ran around with all sorts of weapons. Between this feeling of un-reality and the concentration necessary to draw, I was able to keep my mind on what I was doing—not where I was or what was going on around me. It was only when I was not drawing that I had time to worry, which is one reason I managed to make so many sketches.

I tried to be self-sufficient, living out of my field pack like any combat marine. I wore green fatigues, jungle boots, and marine cap and carried a map case containing several sketchbooks, a paint set with extra materials, some socks and skivvies, plus shaving gear. In addition to a pistol belt with a marine knife, first-aid kit, and two very important canteens, I carried an Instamatic camera, pockets full of film, funny money (MPC), passport, ID cards and shot records, plus enough plastic bags to keep all my sketchbooks dry in case I fell down in a paddy.

In this fashion I then hitchhiked all over Vietnam on any thing that would take me—all kinds of planes, helicopters, patrol boats, mine sweepers, swift boats, Coast Guard cutters, jeeps, and trucks in places like Dong Ha, Phu Bai, Vinh Long, Rach Gia, Soc Trang, and others. I counted my days like all short-timers and it was with much relief when I returned to Da Nang, turned in my funny money, re-packed my sketchbooks and sea bag, put on my wrinkled, dirty but civilian clothes and got on an Air Force jet for Okinawa and Japan, from where I flew home with a load of wounded, drawing all the way. When I touched down at McGuire AFB, I was tanned and happy, 22 pounds lighter, and had several hundred drawings, 30 rolls of film, and thousands of sights, sounds, and smells locked in my mind of a place and of people I will never forget.

I am most proud to have been able to see and record some of the places and people and sights of Vietnam. Some of the finished illus-trations and most of the drawings in this book will find their way into the Combat Art Collections of the USN and USMC. It is hoped that this book of sketches may let you visually experience some of the activities of our fighting men in Vietnam, and perhaps for some, to recall a place, a person, or a feeling once shared.

Charles Waterhouse

"The first thing a very nervous artist ran into after embarking from jet at Bien Hoa was this security guard and his sentry dog crouching in the shadows. 'I don't think I'm going to like it here.'"

"This is my first view of Vietnam—by dawn's early light. It's the bunker check point of the tent camp of the 90th Replacement Bn. Somewhere in the boondocks below the iron triangle, we spent the night filling in forms, turning in cash for funny money (MPC), and waiting for dawn and hopefully a ride to Saigon...'If I can convince the Army I'm an artist and the Navy is expecting me.' There was plenty of outgoing artillery last night— and lots of incoming mosquitoes, too."

"One of the few drawings made in Saigon. A Vietnamese guard outside building where I got plague shot. The GI cans are full of concrete to discourage VC taxi-cabs. The guard has a carbine and bike if he needs them."

"My friend Lt. Bill Savage, Operations Officer at USN PBR Base, Nha Be. He always made sure I had a vest and didn't do anything foolish."

"I made five patrols on PBR's like this one on the rivers of the Delta. Light, fast, fiberglass hull, and lots of firepower."

"Ready to go on my first patrol down the Long Tau River on PBR. They kinda wonder what I'm doing here—me too."

"When we got to this outpost in the Rung Sat Special Zone, the troops of the Army's 347th 9th Infantry were loading LCM's to take them to a new area and keep the Viet Cong off balance. Since this outfit has been in the Delta, the attacks on river patrols have been cut down."

Briefing the General on the Situation Map

"This unit was mortared last night and a large Claymore mine was found about 50 feet from the C.P.—Rung Sat Special Zone."

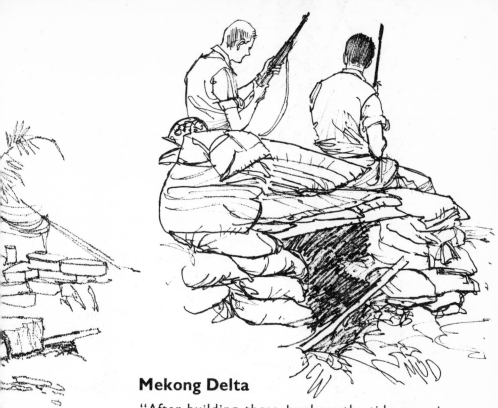

Mekong Delta

"After building these bunkers the tide came in and snakes came out."

"The Vietnamese Navy patrols the rivers in rag-fleet craft like this old French, 10-knot patrol boat."

"Looks like a scene in North Africa, but it's only a muddy waterhole in the Delta where a 105 outfit has set up to support an attack tomorrow."

"This conex box serves as a Vietnamese Navy brig at Nha Be, but the door in the rear is open."

"Lt. C. J. Fagan is salvaging papers and gear from PBR No. 20 which was hit by a freighter and cut in two while on patrol. A beached MSB is in the mud alongside."

Hulks at Nha Be

Sacktime in the Shade of a Seawolf Chopper at Nha Be Pad

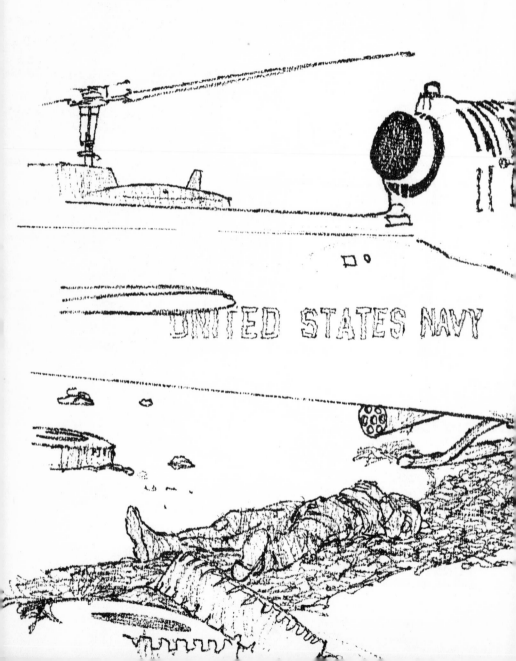

"These Navy men as well as Army helicopter crews are on call at all times to support the river patrols."

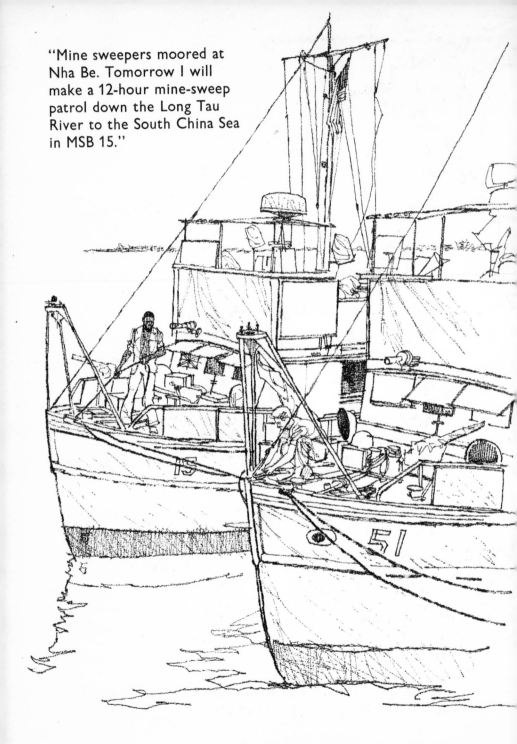

"Mine sweepers moored at Nha Be. Tomorrow I will make a 12-hour mine-sweep patrol down the Long Tau River to the South China Sea in MSB 15."

"Brand" Reading

"They might as well relax because they will never get in the first shot."

"The MSB's keep the shipping lanes to Saigon open."

Mine-Sweeper Man

"The panels are sheets of plastic."

"Sometimes we are only 25 feet from shore...It's spooky."

Chain Drag over the Side

"A mess of spikes and cutters to snap wires leading from shore to contact mines."

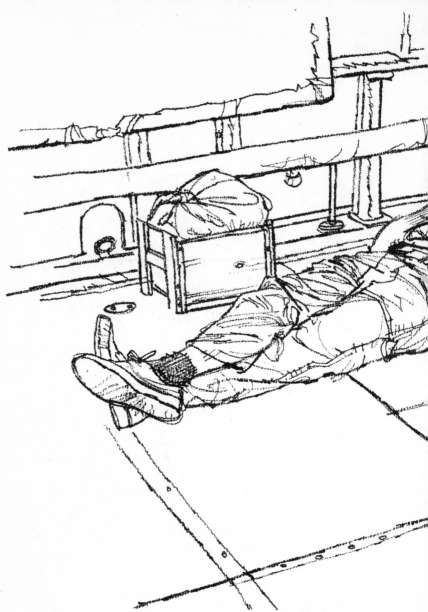

"EM2 Charles Tille, St. Louis, Mo. He may look relaxed
but he's wearing two vests—a plastic one, with a metal
one over it, plus helmet. All crew members on this patrol
are survivors of the boats hit and sunk the day after the
last truce—2 K.I.A. Sixteen wounded, one MSB sunk, one
beached, and two others hit hard."

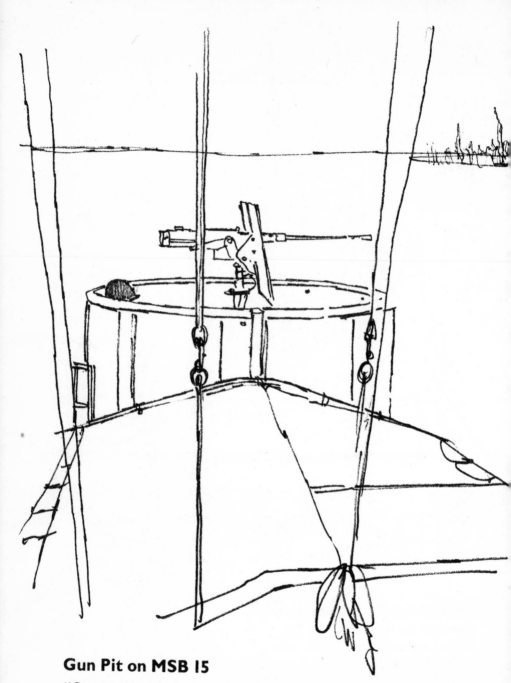

Gun Pit on MSB 15

"On mine-sweep patrol down the Long Tau. Sun is hot."

"MSB 49 was hit and heavily damaged by recoilless rifle fire. Forced aground, refloated, and towed to Nha Be."

"Men of the 199th Light Infantry have just taken this old French fort (1910) in Long Huu. It's got a moat, gun towers, and steel pillboxes. GI's are clearing brush and fire lanes to the sound of tape recorder next to GI eating his C ration."

"The French, Japanese, British, Vietminh, and VC have all used this fort. A rusted French cannon still sits facing the Soi Rap River in this gun tower."

"A large pile of watermines, mortar shells, and other VC gear was captured by 347th 9th Infantry.... The Navy is happy."

The General Is Not Interested in Material

"We even captured a guitar at the VC factory site. A 'friendly village' is about 700 meters away."

"Our PBR is docked at the old French concrete-loading pier at Long Huu. We are getting ready to shove off for Nha Be and will evac Pfc. Pat Meley, 199th Lt. Infantry. His left foot is badly infected from mosquito bites and paddy water."

Hương

"This little Vietnamese lady is employed by the Navy to sweep up the BOQ at Nha Be. Her GI name is Mama San. After posing for me, I asked her to sign it and she took off with my sketchbook while everyone roared as I chased her around the barracks twice to get it back."

"Radar repair on an LCPL at Cat Lo. These boats are responsible for harbor security at Vung Tau."

"Forward twin 50's on PBR and Viet Police Sgt. Long Tau River, Delta. Twelve-hour search patrol."

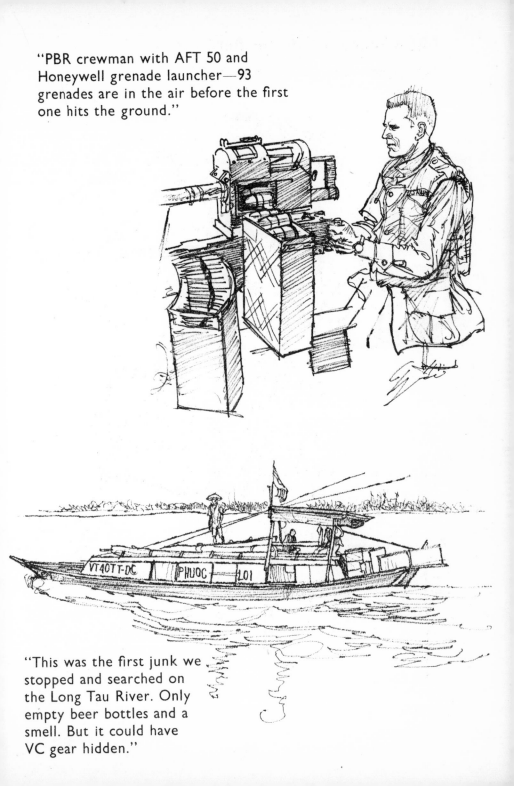

"PBR crewman with AFT 50 and Honeywell grenade launcher—93 grenades are in the air before the first one hits the ground."

"This was the first junk we stopped and searched on the Long Tau River. Only empty beer bottles and a smell. But it could have VC gear hidden."

PBR Lookout on the Soi Rap

"Our planes have just hit something."

"Old Navy" Chief

"... carries shotgun to board and search junks. This man is a tough customer!"

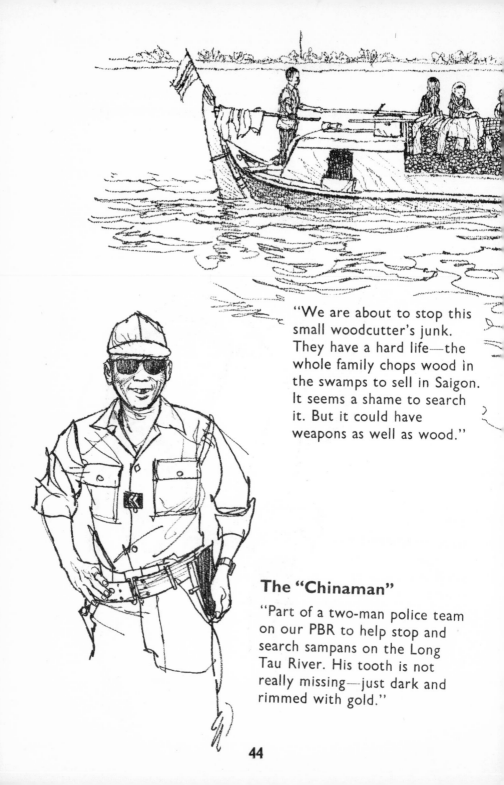

"We are about to stop this small woodcutter's junk. They have a hard life—the whole family chops wood in the swamps to sell in Saigon. It seems a shame to search it. But it could have weapons as well as wood."

The "Chinaman"

"Part of a two-man police team on our PBR to help stop and search sampans on the Long Tau River. His tooth is not really missing—just dark and rimmed with gold."

44

"Sgt. Quyen pokes around with that stick on all the junks we board. He looks salty, and has long thumb nails."

45

Peek-A-Boo

"Sgt. Quyen plays peek-a-boo
on a small woodcutter's junk."

"The only thing below deck is the woodcutter's wife and youngest child."

Searching Junk

"Nothing down there...but it sure stinks!"

"Crewmen and passengers in pilot house of junk we searched during our 'game warden patrol.'"

"Repairing water-jet pumps and holes in the hull of a PBR at U.S. Navy Base, Cat Lo. Fiberglass patches are put on, sanded, and it's as good as new."

"Working on the twin 50's of a Patrol Craft Fast (PCF), or Swift Boat, Cat Lo."

Loading Mortar on Swift Boat—Mouth of Long Tau

"This mortar misfired and exploded after I was transferred to another boat to go ashore. Three men dead, one wounded."

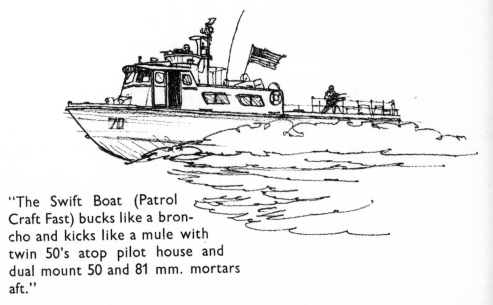

"The Swift Boat (Patrol Craft Fast) bucks like a broncho and kicks like a mule with twin 50's atop pilot house and dual mount 50 and 81 mm. mortars aft."

Two Cooks, Cat Lo—0530

"It's too early to eat so we talk and draw."

"PBR dock at U.S. Navy Base, My Tho in Mekong Delta."

WELCOME · TO

INTERNATIONAL MY-THO AIRPORT

RFIELD ADVISORY NCO AT THIS LOCATION

A ĐIÊN HAS ŬANÐI HÃN PŲ7R ĨNIG

Air Force Operations Bunker on the Small Dirt Strip at Ben Duc near My Tho

"A few ammo boxes filled with sand, a tin roof, and conex box —that's it."

Navy Guard in Bunker at Gate of PBR Base

"Screen protects from grenades and hole gives field of fire. It's daylight or he would wear a vest."

PBR Crewmen at My Tho

"When not on patrol they work on guns and boats. Also sun-burned."

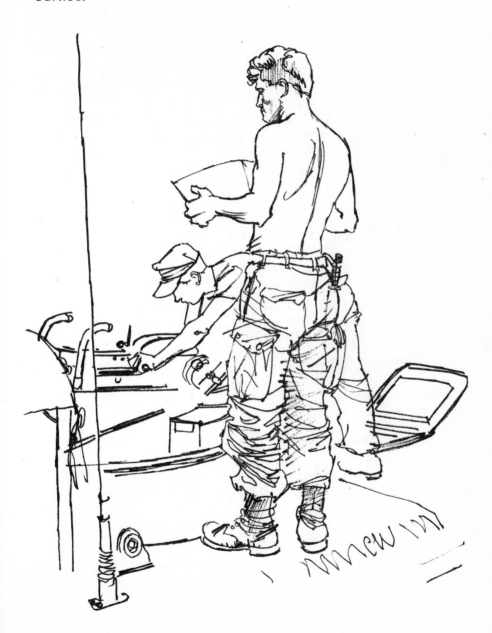

Padre Johnson

"Chaplain Ray W. Johnson, River Assault Flotilla No. 1, with portable altar on his Delta-circuit riding tour. Since this drawing Padre Johnson has been put up for the Navy Cross and Purple Heart for bringing in wounded under heavy fire in the Delta."

The Guard at Old French Victory Hotel—USN Billet, My Tho

"The mess hall is under sign protected by sandbags and bunkers."

Bus Stop, My Tho

"PBR crew outside Victory Hotel
waiting for ride to river and dawn
patrol."

PBR Repair

"PBR out of the water for repairs next to beautiful red-flowering trees along river bank at My Tho in Delta."

Chopper Repair

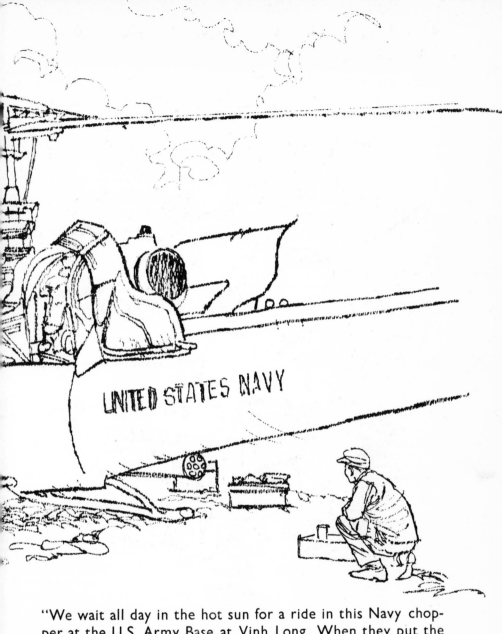

"We wait all day in the hot sun for a ride in this Navy chopper at the U.S. Army Base at Vinh Long. When they put the parts together, we take off."

Spot Jungle Suit—Dark Grays, Greens, Umbers. Vinh Long

"Seawolf crewmen work on the chopper I will go up on. The strip is all stones."

Seawolf Crewman. Vinh Long—Delta

"Black shirt, neckerchief, tight pants, black shoes, gun on hip
—salty."

"Clean the guns at Seawolf Pad. Hot!"

"This man posed for me on the ground. I drew him several times but was so excited over my chopper mission *without* vest or safety belt I forgot to get his name."

Breaktime at the Seawolf Pad

"The discussion is about the number and variety of weapons they carry on missions—phosphorus grenades to Chi Com Burp guns. The pilots worry about all this excess gear, but the gunners delight in it."

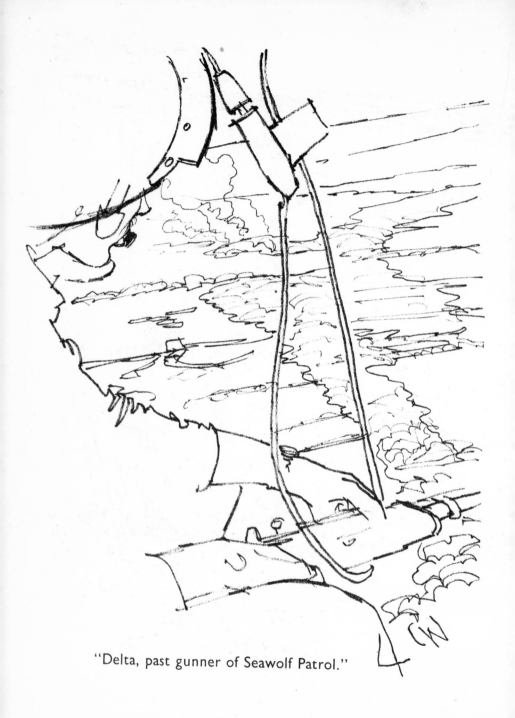

"Delta, past gunner of Seawolf Patrol."

"At dusk these teams went out to patrol the perimeter."

Chapel at Vinh Long

"All faiths hold services here."

"I sat on the
floor of a
Vietnamese
hospital in Rach
Gia and drew
these kids. They had never
seen an artist before—hung all
over me and, for a little while,
I made them happy."

Tran Thi Ha, 71 Years Old, Kiengiang Province

"Black pajamas and red-check shawl."

Muoi Huynh Thi "This little five-year-old Vietnamese girl has lost half her face from a VC mine. In a day or so Cmdr. O'Malley will try to give her a new face with plastic surgery. She has a little bottle in her hand for a toy."

"The little girl's father stood by her side all day to fan and shoo flies. Two of his sons have been killed by VC."

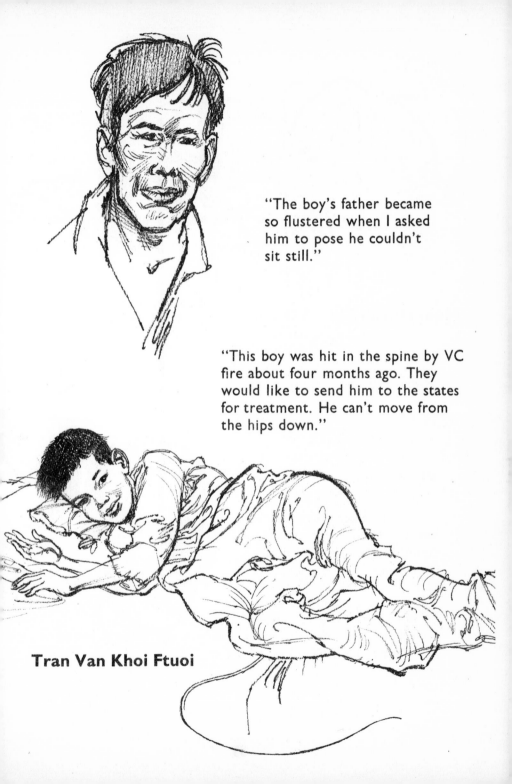

"The boy's father became so flustered when I asked him to pose he couldn't sit still."

"This boy was hit in the spine by VC fire about four months ago. They would like to send him to the states for treatment. He can't move from the hips down."

Tran Van Khoi Ftuoi

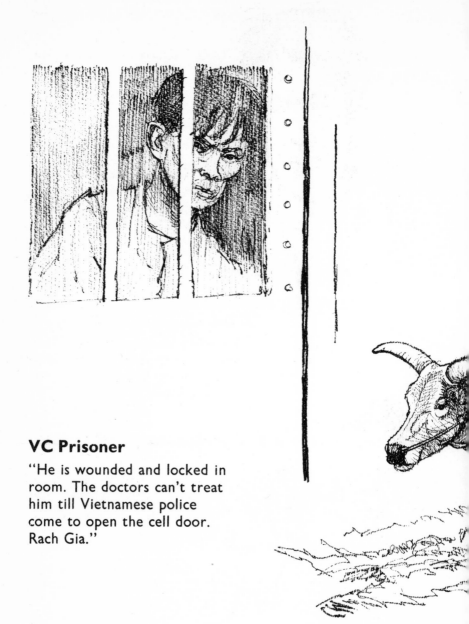

VC Prisoner

"He is wounded and locked in room. The doctors can't treat him till Vietnamese police come to open the cell door. Rach Gia."

"This drawing is from a photo I took from a moving jeep. My driver drove with a gun in one hand and wouldn't stop."

"Pretty Vietnamese with *ao dai* and bike outside the White Elephant at Da Nang."

"It's early morning in Da Nang, and after fixing her hair these river people will be on their way to fish."

"This small Marine observation plane (FAC) is being serviced by USMC ground crew at Marble Mt. The rockets under wing are to mark targets for strikes."

Crapped Out.
15th Aerial, Da Nang

"This could be any place in Vietnam. Everywhere men are sprawled out, waiting for transportation."

"Old French bunker on the perimeter of the USMC 3rd Marine Division combat camp at Dong Ha near the DMZ."

"Combat tent camp at Dong Ha occupied at the moment by the men of Lima Co. 3rd Bn. 4th Marines. They have just come back from an operation at the DMZ. This camp smells of dirt, heat, and war."

"All correspondents, camera and TV men, check in here. MG Sgt. K. on way from day's briefing session."

Press Center Shack at Dong Ha

My Friend & Foxhole Buddy, Phuoc

"He gets to see lots of action as photographer for AP...was wounded trying to capture a VC with knife in one hand, camera in the other."

Gene Young, an Ole Marine

"Works for *Stars & Stripes*. Commutes from Japan to Vietnam every two months."

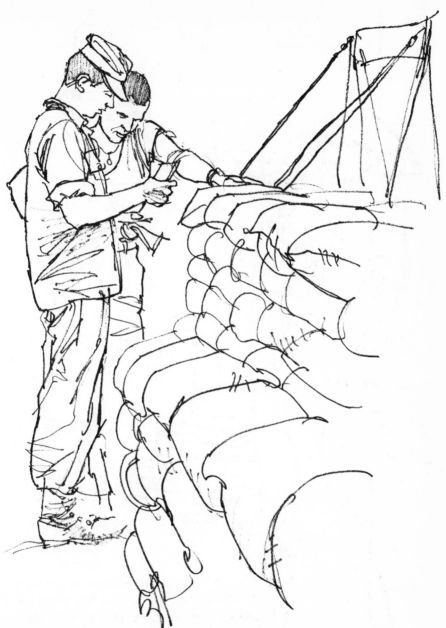

Battery CP 13th Marines, 5th Marine Div. F.M.F.

"I was especially happy to meet this unit as it was the Artillery Reg. of my old 5th Division."

"These Vietnamese women were hurt
sometime last night by a VC mine or
booby trap. Arm of one, neck of the
other. Someone had bandaged them
before they were picked up and
brought in. A Vietnamese TV man is
asking them about it."

"U.S. Navy crewmen cool off over the side of their LCM Mike Boat in a river near the DMZ. The water is dirty, but they look cool."

Car Wash in a River North of Dong Ha on Highway No. 1 to DMZ

"The trucks are pulled into the river and for a few piasters all the kids scrub the mud off."

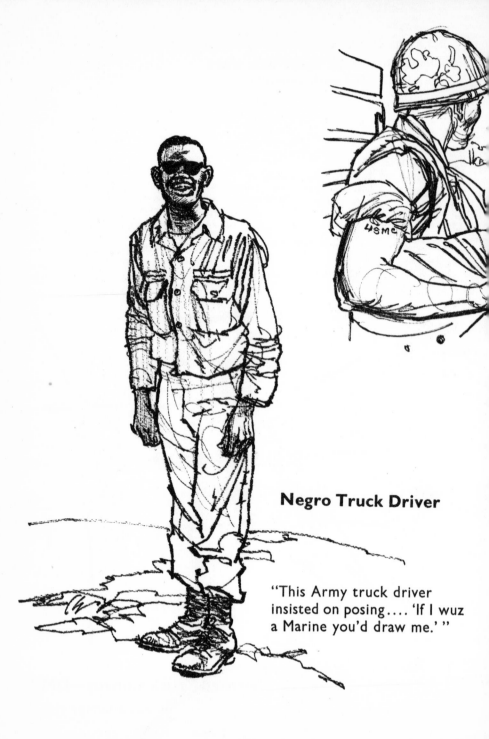

Negro Truck Driver

"This Army truck driver
insisted on posing.... 'If I wuz
a Marine you'd draw me.'"

"I hope that truck keeps back there 'cause it's loaded with ammo!"

Armed Truck Convoy—DMZ

"It was a bumpy ride."

Sampan

"Except for the old French
pillbox on the far bank of this
river near Dong Ha, the war
seems to be faraway."

"On the tank patrol to the DMZ. I expected to ride inside but ended up clinging to the turret like the rest of the Security Platoon. The smoke is from what's left of a seven-truck ammo convoy that hit a mine."

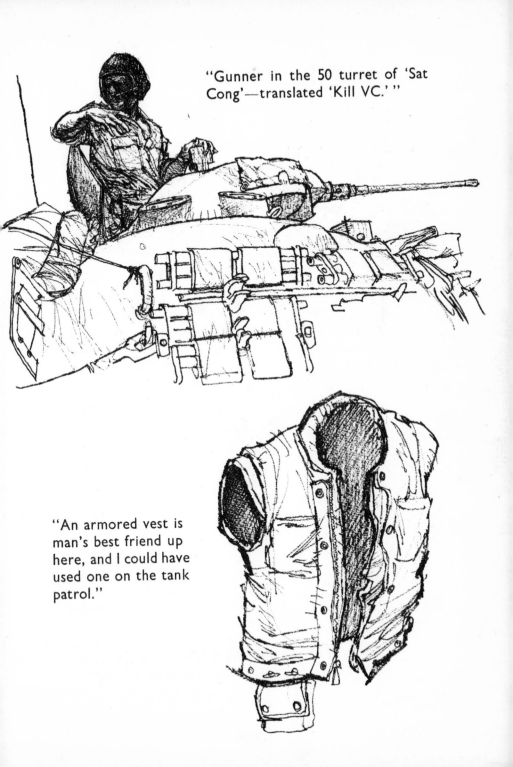

"Gunner in the 50 turret of 'Sat Cong'—translated 'Kill VC.'"

"An armored vest is man's best friend up here, and I could have used one on the tank patrol."

M79 Grenade Launcher

"While we wait for a MED EVAC to pick up a Marine, the Tank Security Platoon spread out into the rice paddies."

Tank Security out in Paddies

"Oblivious to the artillery firing over their heads, a constant
flow of Vietnamese comes down a road near Gio Linh at the
DMZ. Some look like they are clearing out of their village in
background; but most are just on the way to work."

Phuoc

"My foxhole buddy at work on our home at the DMZ."

"We are less than 500 meters from the DMZ—bang bang all around; yet Vietnamese still walk down road in front of our holes!"

"This Marine has just dodged over 500 rounds of VC fire—105-120's. Now it's into the hills to hunt VC."

"U.S. Navy corpsman to the rescue."

"Bringing in the wounded
from the DMZ."

"Casualties are cleaned up and given emergency treatment here and then MED EVAC to the U.S. Navy hospital ship 'Repose' or to Da Nang."

Cracker Box Unloading. D Co. 3rd Med, Dong Ha

"Doctor helping a wounded Marine to the Aid Station."

"The litter cases come first, so they sit quietly and bleed."

"3rd Platoon all Present or Accounted for"

"Bloody and battered equipment outside of 3rd MED, Dong Ha."

Helping Hand

"3rd MED, Dong Ha. The wounded must strip off gear and weapons outside the Aid Station. *No one* is brought in armed."

"And I stand around drawing."

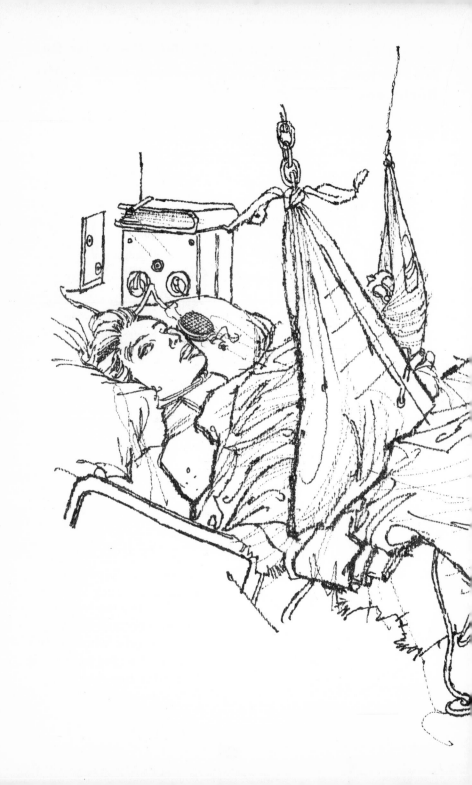

"Good Friday" Cpl. Robert Glodek, Co. C 1st Bn. 9th Marines. Mortar, March 19—Neck, Both Arms, Both Legs

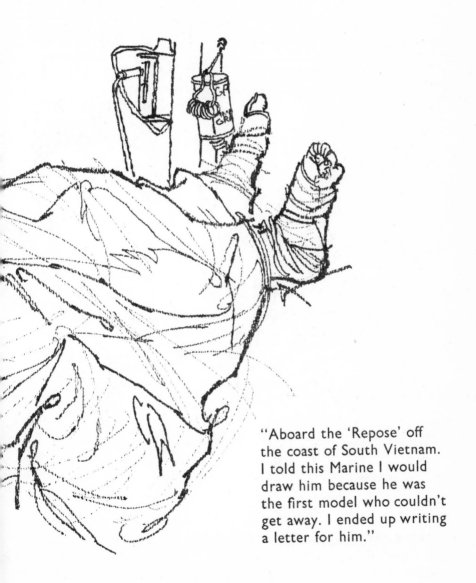

"Aboard the 'Repose' off the coast of South Vietnam. I told this Marine I would draw him because he was the first model who couldn't get away. I ended up writing a letter for him."

"MED EVAC chopper landing on the deck of the 'Repose' off the coast of Vietnam."

"Inside of 20 minutes this Marine litter case will be cleaned up, patched up, tested, x-rayed, and in operating room."

Dead Marine

"To Saint Peter he will tell, another Marine reporting sir, I've served my time in hell."

The End